Calling the Names

Calling the Names

poems by

Mark Saba

*To Sara Underwood
with best wishes!
Mark Saba
5/17*

David Robert Books

Published by David Robert Books
P.O. Box 541106
Cincinnati, OH 45254-1106

ISBN: 978-1-62549-229-6

Poetry Editor: Kevin Walzer
Business Editor: Lori Jareo

Visit us on the web at
www.davidrobertbooks.com

Cover and book design by Mark Saba
Cover photo by Nicholas Saba

ACKNOWLEDGMENTS

Lost Voice in *Poetic Voices Without Borders 2* (Gival Press)

Tree Tectonics in *Steam Ticket*

Reverend Edith on *www.stevebloompoetry.net*

The Year I Didn't Write in *Contemporary Poetry: An Anthology of Present Day Best Poems*

God Lives in the Heart of a Tree in *Literature Today: An International Journal of Contemporary Literature*

for Annie and Nicholas

TABLE OF CONTENTS

Anonyms

Edges

Supplications

Shadows

Anonyms

On Accidentally Touching a Stranger's Foot

On the train from New Haven to Stamford,
a wall of seat backs separating us,
while stretching out my leg

to insert my phone back into a pocket,
I hit something on the floor—a bag,
bear can, or fallen book?

No, it's someone's sneaker, worn out,
poorly laced, pulling back as I look up
and catch his face in the small sliver

peephole. He nods, almost waves,
and I mutter an inaudible "sorry"
before returning to my commuter's

repose. Now we are connected;
I spend the rest of the trip
trying to catch a glimpse of him.

I feel he must be doing the same,
certain that we share a demonstrative
side, a distaste for separation

from our species. He had chosen
the facing seats, after all, while I
kept to my familiar forward-traveler.

At last I see his reflection in the window.
Dosing off? Dreaming? Wondering about everything
I think about on these long trips home?

His eyes are closed, then open; he spies me
too. I look down, away. Why?
I will never know this human.

I could stare right through him
like all the others bleary-eyed
from endless anonymity.

But as I make my way to the door
for my stop I cannot help looking
at him, and he does the same.

Our connection sealed, then broken—
A face I will not remember.
A conversation that failed to save

any bit of our lives.

William Alexander Wimsatt

Whom I've never met, nor ever will
but for the moment I saw his nameplate
on the lackluster pew before me

at 10:30 Mass. I had been basking
in winter windowlight, warm on my head
and back: a wide ray that also hit the tarnished metal,

Gift of the Class of 1968. I'm certain
no one else in the church knew of him
who died shy of nineteen. A freshman perhaps?

I'm sure his parents, if living, are as far away
as their minds could take them
from this refurbished church, this Mass,

their son's name gone anonymous.
I think of the possibilities that may have taken
his life, the pews filled with teary-eyed classmates,

the awestruck priest and trembling servers.
So much is covered up by this church's
cream-colored paint, sublimated expressions

of grief and joy now trailing clouds,
obscuring the etched windows
until the sun breaks through

as each day it must.

To the Young Poet in Pittsburgh
Who Bought a Copy of My Book

What streets you wander, and how you see them
following years of raising yourself up,
may differ from mine. We overlap

only in word, the written and the unwritten,
stories we concoct to paint our own
realities. What I offer is a model

of insistence, a hand to grasp freely
then let go. This city is steeped
in itself, its structures built

upon those tales. Some have burned out
but others await endless translation.
Build therefore the huddled mass

of time. Undo the clock; peel back
the lost curtain. Every construction
begins on the page. Every street

hangs on a name.

Blues

I used to be crazy about blues;
now they don't do anything for me.
I now prefers browns, or red.

I used to lie melancholic
on my bed, wondering
about the people I'd met.

Now I meet them so often
there is no time for
interpersonal rehearsals.

Scarlet cars have always caught my eye
and in my days of blues
I never knew where they went.

Now I drive a red Prius:
Smart, economical, and well equipped
for never-ending duties.

Some say blue bloods
are at the top of the heap
but I prefer being lost

among earthen shades
of skin. Let the blue sky
watch over us.

I'll heed the red call of beating blood.

Halos

In my little boy's dream
two types inhabited heaven:
those who had lived in cities,

he was told, wore halos. The others
wandered in semi-darkness
never sure of why they had lived

but granted the same privilege
of knowing all those faces
at once, strangers

twice.

People Are Dying Behind My Back

People are dying behind my back.

My poet—teacher, who had once entrusted me
to take her lead in class. Gone.

My Italian professor, an emigrant
from Hungarian insurrection. *Addio.*

My father's cousin Alphonse
who wore a top hat as ring-bearer
for my grandparents' wedding. No more.

(In contrast I hear of other deaths
in the news. How insignificant
they are to me.)

My mother's beautiful cousins
who danced with me as a boy
at fire hall weddings. Interred.

Mentors whom I might have contacted
all these years later to boast
of my accomplishments. Gone deaf.

The scores of those who passed
time with me at bus stops,
office desks, cafeteria lines, soccer games.

Where have they gone?

Brief points of conversation
gone awry in time, yet stuck
in the morning air as I awaken.

Birds Without Eyes

I

Someone who I think loved me
contacted me recently, twenty years
later, politely asking whether he'd had

the right email address, apologizing
for such rash behavior. I responded
just as politely, a little unnerved

but just a little, saying I was he.
No, I hadn't remembered
promising to get in touch in twenty years

but yes, I believe I may have uttered
something like that. *How are you?* he said.
I'm fine; I have a family now.

Kids? Yes, two. They are beautiful.
A brief history of his life followed
ending with a stalled, long-term relationship.

We sent each other off with sincere pleasantries.

II

I sit at the dinner table with my wife,
she fiddling with her cell phone,
and notice the pair of blanched

salt-and-pepper shakers
shaped like birds, wings tucked
permanently beneath them, heads turned

in opposite directions. A long history
of flight vanished, and in those complacent
white heads, no eyes.

Loose Ends

Half-hidden by a swarm of six-year-olds
standing on concrete in someone's
backyard: a photograph of me, faded

and poorly scanned, arrives on my computer
from a woman who writes that we were
once classmates. My memory

goes blank. It could be a photo
from someone else's dream: me standing
not quite up to the height of the others,

hands folded behind my back, the sun
in my eyes, but face so welcoming
and at ease. I must have had a nice time

there in that disregarded past, one of many
that never made it into my catalogue
of landmark scenes that constructed me

from a random mess of time.
This unwanted gift has claimed me
wrong. An impostor. Unable to know

the seeds of my self, the one
I have artificially grounded
in the painstakingly familiar,

never the atmosphere of loose ends
that have bound me together.

Calling the Names

We sit and listen
in quiet, tension, acceptance;
an equaling of uniqueness
as they call the names.

In the awkwardness of brutal
precision, their lives line up
despite distant starting points.
They are calling the names.

As they call, we pretend
to listen, hoping for one child
among the many, each of two hundred seventy
called out in slow hurry.

Much as been made of this calling:
speeches, tables set, voting,
faux masterpieces lining the walls,
all in support of the calling.

Yet, as they return to their tables
and the last name is called
the night has already become fog
and traffic jam. Parents return

to detached hovering; the students
prepare for re-evaluation
and nobody notes the triumph
of first kisses and firm rejections

of things not-quite-believed-in
amid the echoes of called names.

A Time Before Names

Saba repeats in three vertical lines
down the war memorial
in my grandfather's town.
No one knows the origin of the name.

Phoenicians lived in Sardinia. So did a band
of Hebrews. Then came North Africans, Romans,
Etruscans. Let's not forget the Spanish
and Catalans. In the Scotch-Irish dialect
of western Pennsylvania they called me *Say-ba*

and figured it for Slovak. If you Google it
you'll find Lebanese, "mackerel" in Japan,
a couple of Finns, and one poet from Venice
who took it as a pseudonym.
Then you'll find the Queen of Sheba

in those biblical stories. Forget
genealogy sites. My relatives?
Dunno. I went to Sardinia.
I've scoured the web, asked everyone
I've met. And all I get

is a blank stare, mirror eyes,
a silence that reaches back to our
dimmest memories, a time before names.

Stretched to the Ends of the Earth

My childhood mined, ensuing school years
analyzed, night-time winter walks tucked away
like portable sparks to light all neutral

sunny days, I have come here
to the ends of the earth—to a Kurdish grandmother
baking bread in an outdoor pit; to an Ethiopian shrine

so holy, only one man may enter;
to an Auckland albatross encircling
the Pacific; to a blind, blanched crab

so deep underwater we missed him
for ten thousand years. To a sunrise
sublimating the ghosts of bloody Mongolian

plains; to the seat I warm in lieu of blanketing
the anonymous with kisses; to the sky, to the August air;
to a backyard creek that carried my footprints

down to the Monongahela, Ohio,
Mississippi, the Gulf, and the Atlantic
before settling into the deep shell

of our planet's core, where I sink
and lie central to anything that may happen.

After Reading Deep River *(by Shusaku Endo)*

After the globe has finished warming
glaciers will have melted from the Himalayas.
In one final gush they will plunge
into the Ganges, which, following its mythical history,
will forever disappear.

The ashes of the dead will dry up
on its shores, as will its offerings
of blinding flowers, its outcasts
floating bloated on the surface.
A river that once used its weight

to push along the sins of the ages,
its silent roar of forgiveness
heard by the masses, painting grayness
over unknowable depths of rights and wrongs
will rise uncovered.

The bones of the unburied will lie
like pale branches on its bottom.
They will bleach under the sun, a tangled mess
of aunts and uncles, whores and lepers,
stateswomen and holy men, children and dogs.

From a satellite image we will see them,
stopped in their eternal tracks,
sins newly unforgiven, creating a glare
that will bounce back from Varanasi
to Kentucky, blinding those of us

who bury the dead in dirt.

Rain Racing

Rain racing down the gutters
nailing the windows and pavement
as it tears at the soft outer shell

of time. So much to be washed away—
relentless in its tearing down
of every beloved second

we have lived. Insisting on blurring
the grandfather in my son's eyes.
Louder than the music of their voices.

Rhythmic in its keen deception,
an endless watery landscape
where nothing outdoes it, nothing outcolors

its gray curtain. It is raining
in every town you have lived,
chiseling those monuments of deepest

time, replacing them with the depths
of unknowable oceans, the runoff
of billions of emptied souls.

Borders

Soon all the world's literature
will fit on an iPod. María Lucinda Cortéz
will read Hamlet in Bolivia
after putting her chickens to bed.

Kirghiz herders will swap Dostoyevsky
for Baudelaire; Lapps memorize Wordsworth
and Uighurs wonder at Whitman.
Perhaps a Tibetan nun will ponder

Emily Dickenson on a long winter's night,
her Little Red Book tucked into a nightstand
as she goes on to the New Testament
and Winnie The Pooh. She will see then not

the Himalayas as she drifts off to sleep
but the whole planet awash in words
rearranging themselves for her amusement
before bumping into her daily chores

the next morning: the wash she hangs
flapping in from seventeenth century Flanders,
tea leaves floating by Gibraltar
on their way to Alexandria.

She sends off a message in cellphonish:
blu poppyz 4 u 2 c below a pic
of their signature flower opening
just for me, but I prefer the smell

of potatoes boiling in my mother's
kitchen, 1967; the reaches of my neighborhood
hemmed in by an unscalable green
and all roads leading out a gentle

narcotic to keep my head bobbing
in the back seat, unaware of a world
at large, where blue poppies pop out
of books to stare at me

then disappear.

Traffic Lights, Keys

On the smooth road
where life is leveled out—
any turn landing us equally—

The unequal glows of green and red
trigger a democracy
unknown to history.

The meek and arrogant,
pompous and pouting
all come to a halt,

wait their turns, sail smoothly
to funerals, interviews, rendezvous
and reunions. The mind frees

as feet work the pedals
and hands turn a compass
steadied by preconceptions.

We've all been rigorously tested,
our vehicles sublimely inspected.
And so this democracy lives

a double life: one the mathematics
of physicists and engineers; the other
a leap of faith that our unknown selves

can meet inconspicuously
if we turn the same key.

Five Hours on a Train to D.C.
Without Opening a Book

I

Because most of the landscape
is unfamiliar, a conversation
I haven't yet had with the gulls,
the jets floating slowly, the planks

making a path through winter marshes
and obliterating ice. We roll by
watching a film where lives
are caught without motion, split seconds

they will never remember; houses they once built
now fallen, wires they once raised
dangling, paths they thrashed
that have taken journeys.

The pageant percolates under a sun
that stares us straight in the eye.
Though we may not look back.
It is only there to show us

what we've been missing, what we'll never see
again so together. For we too are caught
in an uneasy balance: the seeing out
and taking in.

II

Who am I to pretend to know
who lives in those inexhaustible rows
of homes? Each life filled

to the brim of complexity, epics
and tragedies every one.
How many poets are there?

Nurses? Waiters? Tax lawyers? Thieves?
Broken-hearted girls, boys scared as hell
but happily plodding along.

Corporate monsters and monstresses,
musicians, bird watchers, potato peelers, aunts.
Those you've never read about,

forgotten by polls, insignificants
who will never make the news,
the ones we're supposed to trample on

and never admit exist.
Yet they speak today in tongues
on the other side of a moving window

granting me permission to imagine
their brilliant languages, their
songs without words, muffled

but for this pen.

Lost Voice

No more studying languages.
One is enough. Now I seek
not how to say it

but what must be said.
One blackbird, one rose.
One note at a time.

The poets have drawn their
swords, sworn to protect
the earliest phrases

those before Babel, not yet
out of Africa. Vocabularies
might then have been thin

but what have our new words
added? Men still struggle
to say I love you. Women

overflow, but retreat
to touch. New icons now catch
fire: a global campaign

to make up for lost voice.

Escaping America

I can't help it. It's imprinted
in my blood, nourished every cell,
freeze-framed twenty-four by seven
by four by twelve by fifty one times
every morning and sunset, every competitive

moment measured up by those
who molded me, bumped into me,
spoke words that traveled American air
on their way to the deep recesses
of my soul, where they hide in anonymity.

I've spent a life learning
other cultures, first in the World Book Encyclopedias
my mother bought from my father's first cousin
one dreary day as his Italian-American voice
boomed through our widowed house

then as an adolescent in love with anyone
I could not see for the stifling humid air
of our landlocked summers, its tanned women
with bleached hair and men drinking beer
on patios that overlooked other homes

purely Caucasian. The world at large
came only through travel agencies
decorated in overly-saturated photographs
of blue water, white stucco, green and yellow
foods; its history forced through our lens

(never clean) and chopped up
into digestible squares of magic
to validate the money we'd earned.
On my first trip abroad I saw their faces
watching me, full of the same suspicion,

wondering if *America* could really exist.
On returning I found my vision
changed, new colors encroaching
under overpowering light. I wandered from one city
to another, shedding reflections

of worlds that had burned.
Adulthood drew a composite picture
of me, thin outlines supporting a bag
of tricks that wanted out, but solidified instead
into poems and terse prose.

Now I am escaping America,
its history of slavery, selfishness, and blood;
its relentless pounding in my brain
to size up and vanquish, to overcome
my only wish of listening to the secrets

trees bear, the babbling of the living
among our raucous ways, a seed
winging down the rosy evening air
to its unguided destination
where it will undergo a more natural

apathy, one that makes sense only
to the billions of us put together
on nothing but this planet—

oh history of fools
oh songs without borders

that have echoed from the beginning.

Edges

I Live in the Treetops

I live in the treetops,
their gentle movements
welcoming the weather
as it passes through.

I lay myself into
their gentle branches
and they pass me about
the neighborhood.

I return to them on Sunday
afternoons, storm clouds
in the distance, snow falling
through sun. I count

their species, soft firs
and mighty oak. This
is where I can see
both heaven and earth

the before and after.
I welcome the balance.
Yet rooftops
and telephone poles

stay cemented in space
reminding me of future conversations
that must occur—
our intentions

falling from grace.

A Reading

Faces disconnect from voices,
a wash of transparency
under twilight. I give up

trying to find anyone
and wonder if they too are having
this out-of-body experience.

Somehow my voice is lost
under my control. I wonder
whether this does justice

to the moments that I wrote
the text. That too was out of body
but also out of mind, out of control,

out of this world. Seated, applause
inverted, I feel the words falling delicately
around me, landing

on a well-trodden floor.

Voyager

Left our planet in September, 1977
when I was embarking on a career
in pharmacy, one that derailed

within three years. Voyager, however, kept to its
straight and narrow, using Jovian and Saturnian gravity
to help it on its happy way.

I took a different path, transfering
not only my studies but the way I saw
the world. I lay on my bed at the new school

and felt the Earth I thought I knew
swoon beneath me. My past dissolved.
I was marooned in free-falling space

and knew I'd have to reconstruct
not only the world, but myself—
a task not yet completed.

Meanwhile, Voyager 1 continues, breaking out
of the heliosheath, solar wind brushing its back
as it dives fearlessly

into the interstellar medium,
sending signals back in time
to an anxious crew

who are quick to decipher unknowns
clear up to the year 2025, when I may be
winding down as well, dimly aware

that the Earth will soon offer me up
to an empty view.

A Walk with My Teacher in 1979

To reconstruct a scene
from the past, think first of its
color, the way light clamps down

a brown stone wall, velvety green trees,
a woman's honeyed hair, her highlighted
cheeks. The gray road moves beside us

as we walk; students commingle
with the corners of my eyes. Everything, it seems,
is passing by. Think of the shadow

that falls behind, or lurks around
the corner, where no proof exists
for what we must do when we part.

Or no, it is not enough to remember
in two dimensions. Nor her voice,
nor fresh apple blossoms blowing in

from another world. You must gather
these words into your arms,
raise them to your mouth

and devour the page. They must
fall to the heart, like random thoughts
beyond control, that cannot be retrieved.

Homecoming

I drive the distance, the hills, the miles on miles
of angled trees, survivors every one.

I know where I'm going—to a handsome place
packed with other times I've been there.

A good meal, elegant inn, wide beach
of even sand, small birds hiding in the scrub.

I've been there, just as I've been a visitor
to other contentments, even the smug joy

of a day when everything went our way.
Now I am driving toward it—that hunger

for what I already know. It's the very end
of September, yet if anyone would peek inside me

they'd see not a homecoming of greens, golds, and reds
but a bucketful of tears, wherever I go.

Lost in the Light

Walking the rocky shore
its strata strewn diagonally
over an edge of Maine
I wait for autumn to pause

as a winter storm arrives.
The sea is shimmering glass,
its destinations gathered
into a milky luminescence

so I cannot recall
where I've been, where I'll go
after the snow collides with water
and gives itself up. Translucent flames

rise and fall in the hearth
that evening. Borne of nothing
they do not last;
alarming heat and color

recede, leaving only
a darker nothing—fate
too familiar. Our earth
offers a similar permanence,

home for nothings that once had
beginnings and ends. Pausing at the edge
of a continent, the great cloud encroaching,
I straddle longing and fear, flame and ashes.

For now I am lost in the light.

Floaters

Moved or not moved
I sit in one position
head tilted downward

hand brushing the page.
This is the way I record
my life. It has nothing to do

with days, but the floaters
on my eyes, those that wait
for an opportunity to remain

above the biology of death.
Super-vision has its own
vocabulary. It learns only

from itself, keeping me
somewhat distant
yet keen to discover

its motile syntax
its insurmountable pull away
from the constructs of common sight.

Things I Almost Bought

A yellow VW, '78, like a sunrise
riding through gray mud.

Then the black wagon, '49
sold by a farmer near Roanoke
who had kept it in a barn so long
it looked as though it had crawled
though a wormhole of time—
the best five hundred bucks
I never had.

For thirty Marks
I could have had a whore in Hamburg
but my hostel mate from New Zealand
tugged me away. Several times

I've held the more expensive bottle of wine,
read its stellar review, and set it back
onto the rack as those little bottles of exotic liqueurs
eyed me from behind the counter.

Might a simple brushed brass earring
have looked nice in my ear?
Or a black leather jacket
matched by a wide-brimmed hat?

By now I'm guessing I'd prefer
to go naked and barefoot, drinking water
on my way to holy shrines
where everything looks unholy and deranged

full of others just like myself
but with more exotic props
whose values diminish, the closer I get.

The Year I Didn't Write

The year I didn't write
I wrote: on the backs of envelopes,
yellow sticky notes, loose sheets torn

from their pads. I wrote notes
at the soccer booster club meeting;
notes to stick on the doorway to see

as I was leaving; lists of what
to fix, buy, or investigate.
I wrote much in my head as well——

Grandiose plans for another novel
percolated along with confessions
meant for no one, designs for

a better life, words to awaken shapes and colors
in my next painting. In short, words
tumbled over words and phrases

that never left me, leaving me to wonder
whether what I had written was real,
and which was better: the manuscripts

sitting coiffed in their bound books
on my shelves, or the steady flow
of unaltered utterances, pure as

India ink, permanent in their own
right, the year I didn't write.

When I Come Home

I

When I come home
doesn't matter if it's been a day
or a month, seems I've been gone

a lifetime. The furniture looks
unfamiliar, like a distant cousin
who's grown another life.

My duties of feeding the cat
and taking out the trash taunt me
so that I have to learn them all over.

The rooms grow together
in anonymity; light from many windows
washes out the lovely moments

I should be remembering, the ones before
we had Italian leather couches
and a cleaning lady. When I come home

nothing is the way I remember it
not even the bananas in their bowl
nor the view from the back window

where so many trees have changed—
grown, fallen, or over-reached their yards;
all their leaves invisible, a compost

that brews year after year.

II

One day I'll come home to find
my garden devoured by fungus and bugs;
winter will bring only dust, not snow

and fall will arrive in one shade
of gray. One day I'll find
that all of my favorite songs

have disappeared without a trace:
no stereo, radio, ipod, or great aunt
humming tunes in the kitchen.

One day all will be well
with my family: no quarrels, disease
or jealousy. No grudges or misunderstandings,

no waiting in a hot car in a traffic jam
nor soccer practice at 6 AM.
One day I'll look up and find

not the omniscient sky, but a cold lid
studded with artificial lights.
The trees will come down, uniformly,

one night as I sleep, and the oceans
drain of salty beginnings. In their place
I'll find, one day when I come home,

that there never really was an Earth,
just a stack of memories floating
off, leaving us as empty shells,

passive voice, useless eyes
and an unlocatable heart.

Damariscotta

(for Annie and Nicholas)

Was the town where we bought fish
for an Italian fish stew
which we cooked in a lovely cottage

set back amid the pines, its screen door
offering us a mottled view of Maine lawn
in sunny September. We walked on rocks

at Pemaquid Point, our daughter in tow,
letting the waves break at our feet.
Twenty years later there is so much more

to discover: each peninsula furred by its own
flora and history. We tour a recovered settlement
of English adventurers, survey a fort built

to guard things never seen, watch the water
harbor heartfelt hues. We find there
a future intensely intricate, landscapes

to tame our opened hearts, our emptiness
for having let go a daughter
and now a son, those two unknowns

we nurtured into mysteries, our lives
entangled like the seaweed
that appears with the falling tide.

Castaway

Riding the tip of rush hour,
diesels and flatbeds pushing me along
two-laned Route 34, I quit its curves

for the wide-brimmed interstate, humming acoustic
to put me at ease. I pass those exiting
for bigger places, dreams only they

can scale, and end up on a highway
flanked by hills, autumn-tinged,
mostly to myself. Hudson Valley

spreads below, quieter than a lifetime,
a premonition of smaller roads
that lead to my destination.

My daughter rides a train simultaneously
coming from another direction,
a campus overpopulated by desires,

a time so full she barely offers
an embrace: she who doesn't know
I've skipped out of work early

to find this peace on my way to fetch her
and meet the chaos that resides
in a far-flung piece of us.

Bowdoin College Commencement, 2014

(after Martin Buber's *I and Thou*)

The first day equals the last
but for the ferns breaking through
four winters, the black-throated green warblers

flashing by cedars, and eiders defiant
in their black and white robes. The graduates,
meanwhile, applaud their professors

after walking the throng-filled quad,
some with white ribbons to remember the dead
others stepping gently over ghost tracks

laid by themselves. Choreography
becomes possession, as does the past,
and parents offer nothing but tenderness;

for what they see will lie in state
somewhere between past lessons
and floundering advice for a world

imperfectly defined. What they want
is to forget, but cannot, the images they've held
of their sons and daughters, replacing them

with a knowledge that comes disrobed,
that shares a sense of being and not
direction, that becomes not the view

of the changing water, but the currents
that pull past from present
and keep us from knowing either.

Going in Circles

(after Jackson Pollock's *Number 13A: Arabesque*)

I'm going in circles
buried under Earth.

Circles point the way to sounds
in my head. Combine them with sticks

and full stops, drops
that sputter, bleed, bang.

See where they lead: to whole worlds
of what we've located, then strung

together. Stories we tell
then re-imagine in two dimensions.

Pietàs. Pastorals. Portraits.
It unsettles us to know them so.

Centuries of retelling deaden
the message, trap us into believing

we've made peace. But no,
it's back to what begat us—

A motion of Earth's rotation.
The underlying alphabet

of paint.

Star-Shaped Balloon

Child of Mylar technology, precision cut
above Christmas cookies, it rises silver
in pre-storm air——the hand that let go

invisible——a star above antique stores
and upscale warehouses, but little human
activity at 6 PM. Making dinners,

suffering exercise, proposing marriage,
we miss the guiding shape we've created,
content that it should speed away

to its appointed destination
then melt into the evening sky
alongside its more distant cousins

as they trumpet their existence
and offer us, once more,
their patient patterns, polished

navigation, freedom from captive
imitation.

Hanging the Mirrors

One's a new antique, taking up the length
of our buffet. It might have hung
in a mid-century hotel, home to the faces

of postwar brides and soldiers still shy
of seeing themselves so bared again.
The other, more modern, gave my daughter

a thousand check-ups pre-party, pre-date,
pre-parental collision. I hang them now,
along with one other, in the wide space

we now call home. Not used to so many
reflections, I care not to note how steadily
they record our every movement, their infinite recession

of indelible images drinking in
our lives. They will have the last say
no matter what illusions we may live by.

Then again, when we look at each other
we include all the places that didn't
record us, nor our marvelous follies

so we are free to recreate them
in the glass of reflecting eyes.

Grays

Points distant
on an aerial map of Pittsburgh
delineating neighborhoods, those I traveled
ante-Google: birthplaces of my mother
and father, my young-adult love,

the city's edge where I worked at Halboth's Pharmacy
and stared down the enemy Carrick boys.
From here it now looks so blatant
as if those colored shapes had been
pieced together by a bored Creator

on a Sunday afternoon. *Look at me.*
I'm traveling by car in a twisted urban landscape
before engineers and city hall
could smooth it out, ease our connections
and demolish the past.

The cemeteries lie hidden
like emeralds, unbudged amidst the exodus
of each generation, whose tight fabrics
hang in the air, steel threads
entangling the neighborhoods

in their shades of gray.

No Outlet

(for my mother)

I walked the snowy streets of a childhood
long gone, their lengths decreased by anxious steps,
predictions I hesitated to believe

before arriving at the common home, her room
tucked away down the hall, a window overlooking
an empty field, bare trees, three mourning doves

and a sky that slowly grew stars.
Her breathing kept pace with her heart,
first heavy, then light, as the hours

coalesced, a vigil we kept
until the morning she died, and I couldn't tell
if the last few days could be called life

but for her eyes always open, refusing
to miss an instant of her time there
on that street I used to reach with my bike,

the one with no outlet.

I Feel My Heart May Give Out
at Any Moment

On waking, the palpitations
of dream and day colliding

keep me wondering if I will make it
to the shower, where hot water rolls

down my scalp and back, calling me
to arms. Today I've lost an hour

to early March. My clocks fare better
at the adjustment. I just go my way

foregoing the lousy news for sappy
morning classical. Along the route to work

I hum, sing out, anything to keep off remembering
those who have left me too focused

on a stammering heart, aware
that it contains a finite number

of beats, not knowing
how many I've kept to myself.

My Journal Stops

(for Joan)

My journal stops—
descriptions of Copenhagen, Stockholm,
Leningrad, and Warsaw come
to a halt; the Austrians I met

eating cake in Gdańsk, the metallic water
running by Chopin's house, clouds that blended
Lithuania with Mazuria. A record of change
comes in perspective: how Hamburg

reinvented itself, Brussels crowded me out
by extravagance, Moscow through lace curtains
at 3 AM. What was this landscape
I was thinking? The need to burn it

into words? Life will never be
so organized, and mostly pass
unwritten. My journey stopped
with you. Screens dropped; cameras

fell to pieces. My pen ran out
and paper disappeared. The days we spent
defied capture; the anti-world
of our reality posed no language

but the one we engendered
before it flew away, leaving us

scorched by a love that utters
its own vocabulary, transparent,

elusive.

Being One Place but Wanting Another

Twenty-five years later, the story in my head
replays its emblematic frames
without connections. I see only

the stone house, two cows in the yard,
our sentimental host whose musty inn
kept a large portrait reproduction

of JFK. How we got there was unimportant.
I only know we were at the edge of town,
the edge of foreign unknowns

whose uniqueness had settled in us.
Today we meet an old woman
dressed in a pink sweat suit

and sneakers just as sporty
though she seems to have trouble
walking her age in them.

A smudge of rouge on each cheek,
small umbrella shielding the sporadic
rain, she jumps to tell us

about the builder who leveled the yard,
covered the stone with a pebbled façade
and barely spends any time there.

The picture frightens me
because now I know its place,
the way that leads to and fro,

its spotlight in a well-lighted,
new town. I prefer the darkness
of my thoughts, the emblems

distilled there: the place where two frail adventurers
locked themselves together, then set out
on winding Connemara roads

under uncertain skies.

Twenty-Five Years Ago

On the bank of a high road
lightly traveled, an anchorage
for wild fuchsia and stone

light got caught in our eyes.
We noted the disappearance
of befores and afters: we stood

in a tiny graveyard, face-to-face
with time, its signature
brushing our feet. Where would we go?

Too many visions intruded
but Ireland gobbled them up
and left us marooned

in evergreen. And so we became
one, reflecting passing clouds
so that all light poured into us

and rested in that quiet place:
the place of no befores and afters.

Allegheny Airport

A summer of thunder and lightning
clears the air, keeps our gardens
green, but sends us to the edge

where expectations meet the unknown,
feelings exploding on the far side
of decision. We are interrupted.

By now we should be used to it.
After all, very little of what makes us
comes from the gentle spring. Storms

tend to grind us, keeping us shocked
and attentive. Every peel of thunder
brings me back to Allegheny County Airport, 1960

supported by my father's arms, catching breath
as military jets take off and land,
filling a toddler's guarded air

with a noise that had no direction,
a premonition that I would one day
be propelled there, alone

in the thrill of my unfolding.
For within one year he would be gone.

A Death in the Family

I don't know how he did it
so calm at the end of May
when the hillside darkened

with life, the air emptied
of effort, and others let go
of winter's wear. He must have

given half of him to us, who stayed
in the roles we'd been granted.
He must have seen the balance there

and thought nothing could wrong it,
not even his absence, like spring rain
falling on dormant ground

and gone into a future wild
with certainty. I don't know how he did it,
my mother sitting there untouched,

a vision of love unfinished, all their days
gone gray. It must have been right
to tie a long line to the future

and leave one end in him.

What Might Have Been

I open the gray cardboard folder, and inside
a wedding photo—my parents
looking shocked but strangely relieved

of the lives they are leaving.
I think I've never seen them so young,
age-reversed as I grow older,

but now they are both gone
the photo tells a different story:
what might have been had he lived

and my past supported by an elusive
whole. What house might we have
had, what neighbors, what modicum

of American normalcy, instead of my
wishful reconstruction of their everlasting
youth? I put the folder back

into a dusty box. My children will have
little interest in them, a black-and-white
already going gray—

a whorling cloud that joins so many
others. I've tucked their love away
so it goes to earthly pieces

as I tuck myself into bed, and lay my head
on a cardboard pillow.

Too Much Is Made of Dying

Too much is made of dying—
a simple blow to the head,
an ending, endorphins racing
to cover up the bloody details
and pageantry of grandiose exits.

It's more the living that pains us,
that stains our consciousness
and hums a funeral dirge
to prepare for endings unknown.

Too much is made of last words,
the gathering of intimates guarding
a final breath, when a trail of exhalations
colors the globe like a garden
of heavenward flowers, grounded weeds.

We would do better to look
the other way when death finds us,
for its blow will be swift
and most unlike the sting of life
when all we knew was the pendulum of pain
swinging from love to solitude again.

One Quiet Drop

The esteemed academic wrote a book about religion,
making fun of it, proving our imbecility
in concocting it, citing the evil

it has perpetrated. Logically, then, we should
be done with it. We have secularism
to take its place. No need to reach back

to spent lives, nor wonder at the minds
who created mandalas and pietàs.
Forget about martyrs, or those who consider

why they were. And I know this is shaky territory
but disposing of human remains would be much simpler
without the perpetual pomp. Feeling bad

or confused? Buy something. Still unsure?
Buy more. Questioning existence?
It's a joke. Spend an afternoon watching

old family movies—blinding lights
in grayscale, strange gates and uneven
smiles. The dead could have been gone

forever, but here they are, grand uncles
and aunts, elderly neighbors and marked
young, all resurrected by technology

as you sit stone-faced, happy and sad
to see them again: one quiet drop
to make your vase overflow.

Recovery

It's hard to find a good candle.
One that doesn't drip, smoke, or go up
in flames. One that burns as slowly

as a summer day. One that throws off
a delicate scent, like a grandmother's
hands. One that holds steady

making you wonder about the duality
of fire. When you blow it out
its wax reforms the handiwork

of bees, a gentle whiff of steadfastness
and confidence. There are varying degrees
of religion: the one that slaps you in the face,

another that imprisons your soul,
and the third that burns through the ages
holding its fire in check

offering slow recovery.

Making Room for the Archbishop

In a crowded hallway of parents,
students, teachers, and toddlers
Sister Mary Grace ready
to pluck her guitar
before the pedestaled blue Virgin—

A podium posturing to dwindled
multitudes, fed by the ever-squealing
amplifier; large print opened, ready
to be pointed at by the red-robed

assistant—He waddles in like a duckling
grown but not growing, white hair unstuffed
from his lamé bishop's hat, and takes

the lowly stage. He reads like one
under his years, large ears measuring
the attentiveness of this flock, before the Monsignor
shoos us away from the staircase

and we watch him take his hurried, studied
steps up the rampart to bless
the school's newest rooms.

We must wait
until his image has been redrawn
in foundations of air, the newly emptied steps,
before following him up to our storehouse

of vacant imagination.

The Last Snow

Every snow has it story
built on accumulations of annoyance,
tardiness, backaches, despair.
Boldly beautiful is one, as is

a leftover mountain of icy dirt
stuck in a sunny day in May.
The last snow is different.
Unannounced, it falls on green.

It's hard to be mad at its delicate
lace, soon to meet an untimely death,
leaving only a memory of snow
as elusive as wood nymphs

playing in morning fog. The last snow
outlines life as well as death
in one continuous stroke.
We accept it from the corner

of our eye, careful not to wink
lest it betray us the following year.

Reading Elizabeth Bishop in Saint Martin

The cricket in the corner silenced,
air conditioner keeping watch
from its sub-ceiling perch,

the room aglow in afternoon's
pinks and mints, balcony seen
only through shut glass. That tropical world

goes uncontrolled, like memory.
I sit on the white-covered divan
next to the only lamp, reading

as if taking part in last season's dream.
Her words filter the air,
catch the movement of Caribbean warblers

fluttering silently by bougainvillea. I call out
and receive an answer—a cow lumbering
along her childhood's Nova Scotian road,

or mouse spying her over its back
as it leads her through autumn woods
on her way to becoming herself.

The tropics give no answer
only a brief illusion of time,
a calling card whose appointment

is never kept. I wish for the cold dark
of years, a teacher who hands me
a solipsism that calms,

that endures because of its bravery
in a world of too much color
where only a pair of arresting eyes

can throw us off course.

Tree Tectonics

A thrash of oak, windswept pine,
quivering cedar, and dogwood dashing
before all others: each species inhabits

its own plane, airy universe, rhythms
peculiar to the shape of leaf, weight
of branches, density of season.

We watch from inside a sealed window.
Storms coming? Or do they rehearse
scenes from their own demise? Great sheaths of life

call our attention, surrender their souls
to movement, however unpredictable,
like continents adrift in our

backyard, ready to form new
allegiances, new swirls of violent
complexity, each chaos the more beautiful

against a show of others.

Leaves Scratching the Surface

Leaves scratching the surface
of concrete, their metal points
unable to break through limbo,

cast-offs at the end of their lives,
they have no where to go.

Some will skim down to the parking lot
to spend the winter huddled
in jagged balls of rust and brown;

others will get stuck in crevices
at the underpass.

By spring they will have lost their souls
to the footsteps of weary walkers
and the lights of budding trees.

Then they will disappear
in the daggers of rising weeds

and the currents of opposing winds
that lift them back into the sky
and tear at what is left.

Supplications

Tethered

Evening comes. First
the geese pass, then
the great horned owl
coos across the street.

I open my eyes to see darkness
encroaching at the window,
the room still, Omar the cat
asleep at my side.

I re-awaken, never sure
of whether I've left
or what I'm coming back to.
Tethered by half-sleep

and future plans, I meet the ghosts
of both. One sucks my breath away.
The other plays a distant melody
I must leave to re-live.

Hearing Things

Now, at 50, I'm beginning to hear things
in the pause between conversations,
amid the notes of Philip Glass's *Mad Rush*

played by my son on the piano,
creeping about my attic as I fall
asleep, caught in my wakeful ears

as others sleepwalk about. Here is a voice
that whispers what we want to say;
there is a cue I find only at certain angles

or rifts in the air where such things
dwell—ancestors, missing persons, missed
opportunities, choices that flickered once

then burned to the ground. Now
I skirt oracles on my way to Mass,
turn my head when the wind lifts

my hair, pause at windows
cracked open. So much has this world
to tell, and I've spent half a century

missing.

The Dishwasher and I

We meet at 3 AM, the dishwasher
and I, he in his steady hum
working diligently, giving me a wink

of red pinpoints in darkness.
I have come for a glass of warm milk,
dash of honey, a cracker or two

and long look at the moonlight
on the other side of a window.
This is the world that makes up

half our lives, our work
never complete, a suffocating silence
that lays our thoughts bare,

rarely retrievable in daylight.
I envy the dishwasher's confidence
in completing his task, while mine go always

undefined. At dawn I return to meet him,
his door warm but the motor
still. Outside, in the depths

of my yard, a barred owl sits
in harmony with a long branch,
his eyes two drops of void

intent on drinking in another day's shadows.

Salvos

For days the old air brushed
my cheek. Weeks. It hung heavy
with appointments, familiarities.

It brought phantoms from other
months. Years. Dark chiseled ice
that caught in my throat.

A body numb from air of equal
definition, I didn't know
if I moved in thoughts I'd conceived

or future echoes of a voided past.
Then came the deer at 3 AM
breaking branches as others slept.

I felt a cool shiver about me.
New spirits came breathing past,
silent salvos at my cheek.

Full Moon, All Saints, Lauds

"Some we know are already there,
while others may not have reached it
yet. That is the difference between All Saints' Day

and All Souls'." A bright, round light travels
through a dark, cloud-shrouded sky.
We approach small lights on a hill to sing-in

the day. The monks order past; we have taken
our seats, opened the psalters. A last demon escapes
through a hole in my dreams as the psalms

fill my mind, sung slowly, building line by line
small fortresses in us. We take them
on our way as the Moon falls out of the sky.

We have an hour before the sun comes up
to go back to dark rooms where
our ancestors wait, hungry for light.

Catching Light

We've all caught hail, snow,
falling plums and ping pong balls.
But who knows what happens into hands

while we're listening for the score,
looking for a face, awakening?
Here comes the resplendent astronomer

now taking a break from her work
of finding other worlds. Instead, she supplicates
an antique telescope pouring light

downward, and catches it in upturned hands.
She looks into a bowl of condensed
universe, a gift reversed

by an old machine. For a moment
she knows exactly what she's caught;
the rest revolves around a domed room

covered by a quilt of distant, pinholed sight.

Flames

Sooner or later
days fail. Years
compress, none
determined. Calendars

are no longer worth the paper.
Resumés lose translation.
And classroom hours
melt into night.

Each alarm clock,
datebook, certificate, degree,
birthday card, Christmas kiss,
flower bed, suit, and haircut

goes down the tubes.
This Real Life floats
out to sea. Left
are a host of impressions

that refuse. One
may be an exotic meal
prepared by a pretty aunt.
Another, the point

at which you stopped
devouring childhood books
and stepped instead
onto the long road

of daylight, where visions
would no longer be playthings
but markers
that engulfed you in flames.

Reverend Edith

In 1985 or thereabouts
my mother visited Reverend Edith
who saw through time. She lived

in the dirtiest part of town
under a belching steel mill. First
she held my mother's hand

and together they said the Our Father.
My mother, who must have recited it
ten thousand times, said she felt

every word
for the first time. Reverend Edith
looked at my mother, told her

she had a sister who had passed,
a husband too, then a few words
about each of her children. One

was very thin, and worried. He lived
far away. *But you tell him not to worry,*
because in April the heavens will open up

and he will become very successful.
I waited daily. I lost my job,
had no place to live. No one

to hold me. It was April.
Things got worse. By the end of the month
I was sure it had been the worst time

of my life. I've been waiting for Aprils
ever since, and they have come and gone
twenty-seven times, taking all their

beauty with them, leaving me sneezing
in May. But today, April 10, 2012
I found myself staring out the kitchen window

unable to get excited about anything
but the red quince bush and weeping cherry,
the flicker who had just returned,

and the warmth of my body
against the cold reason of humans,
their bow to tyrannical time.

Cocoon

Feeling now as if I could dive
out of my skin, remove its layers
like years, circumstances

I could erase, and be everywhere
exposed finally for what I am,
I sat in the garden room and felt

a cocoon of sunlight tuck me in,
pin me back in place
to this dangerous time, and give me

a new history of self-containment
that is really something like courage:
a flight without wings, and just as good.

Grass

I

It began on Mathilda Street
one holiday gathering, rooms so full
I was lifted from one to another

then set down in a grandmother's
lap. Tomato sauce and anise scents
tickled my senses, but she provided

the Italian sun, a potpourri of her
homeland's landscape transplanted
to a Pittsburgh home, and I fell asleep

in her fragrance, a clean
more providing than taking away.

II

I recognized cut chick
weed, the soft bend of chicory,
understated Queen Anne's lace.
Once I tasted dandelions.

III

I lay on chilled sand,
seaweed stranded in browns
and greens at my feet.

Somewhere, the sea grew life
and threw the rest at us.
Dented shells, opened clams

and salt spray no matter what;
beginnings and endings that swirled in the breeze
combing my terrestrial body

as if to beg forgiveness
for sending me off. But I was
there, sea-bathed and sun-dried

refigured into the scene, deconstructed
into salt-scent and sand,
my arms and toes pressing imprints

into their antediluvian code.

IV.

Before becoming a man
I knew them by smell.

My grandfather smelled like
beer/snuff/cigars.

My dead father was a bottle
of Old Spice in the cabinet.

Certain uncles
seemed to sweat sweets.

My friends on the track team—
we were all in it together.

And my philosophical friend
at Wesleyan, who grew conversations

that lasted well into the morning,
who wore an uncut beard

and accepted the rain along with
the sun, who reached above the Earth

for something above us, I would say
he smelled like grass.

Lovely

Lovely the moment I awaken
from early evening mid-sleep,
my bones resettled, breathing

out of control, to remember
how it was I once lived as a widow's
child, how a stark November

uncovered the bones of weeds,
seed pockets now the graves
of spiders, empty nests adorning

the vast tangle of grape vine.
Lovely that old perspective
of neighborly yard, six or seven

microworlds of rhubarb, asparagus,
pear, apple, and cherry; of long-needled pine
and rose blooms defying their thorny

nature, an old woman on a porch
surrounded by carpenter bees,
her white clapboard and windows framed

by a green I would one day paint.
Lovely the sun that scorched my neck
as I bent over picking peas

or beans, the furry tomato leaves
spreading their unmistakable scent
over my hands, the broccoli coming up

straight, dried blood spilled around
to keep rabbits at bay. Lovely the nest
of newborn garter snakes twisting over

one another, curling about my wrist,
and the obscure Italian sports car
passing by the back ally.

These are the loves of my life,
the first half now gone,
our planet now imperiled.

Lovely the adulation
of time, its seconds recorded
in perfection, its gifts a deck

of cards to play, reshuffle
and deal around the table
in solitaire, every last one of them

a prize.

Small Hands

Small hands
moving over dirt,
shaping a world bound
by nothing—

smoothing out roads
and dusty curbs, driveways
and cul-de-sacs
for Matchbox cars.

I line up leafy twigs
to line the streets,
make garages from their boxes,
run the cars over my shirt

to keep them clean.
This world is two steps
from our cellar door.
It slopes steeply

from our busy street
down to a patchy yard
shielded by a foundation
that supports a trembling old garage

not as nice as the ones I make
for a motor world
that colors the gray dirt
with Chevys, Buicks, and Pontiacs

all neatly parked
but ready to go anywhere
if I prepare the way.

Wide Strokes

Half a century ago I rambled about
Dolly and Russ's house on a sloping
Mount Oliver street, their back door
leading to the alley where my mother parked.

She sat at the kitchen table with Dolly
drinking coffee while Russ showed me
his tropical fish, and I would lose myself there
among the shadows of their long house

as my brother and sister played with their
age-related Nowowiejskis. The backyard
was concrete, but Dolly put a few flowers
here and there among the pigeons

and Pittsburgh air. I jumped down
their thirty steps to Jucunda street, where once
someone was raped as their oldest daughter
watched from her bedroom window.

But the fish tank and boiling kiełbasa
and creaking floors and *Busia* who lived mostly
upstairs enveloped me in a protective sheath
of warm indifference to anything I might find

in future years. Entrusted to figure it all out
I knew, even then, that it would be
a big job, though the palette was clear
and my brush ready for wide strokes.

Between

The ghost of a boy
opening up to manhood—
hair flying, spirit dreaming,
traveling the winds of desert,
forest, and mountain pine—

Not knowing how fragile his condition,
taking stock in seconds
to fill a basin of time.

I see him now at the edge of a city,
his lean purpose a mirage on the road, equal
to my reflection in the narrow mirror.

He only looks at me when I look away
but oh, how beautiful he is! How selfless
in his quest for self! He speaks

in saguaro semaphore, reflects his will
on the backs of quiet mountains.
His brow is the russet earth
he has just inherited. He says

it's okay to bring him home, to dwell
in my time as well, to be
what he has become.

Sending My Son to Barcelona

An unpredictable crick in my knee
has me ascending stairs sideways.
My usual running gait has been reduced

to middle-aged, measured steps.
I get to where I need to go, no
further. Dreams of wild adventures

in foreign lands now percolate
in the been-there, done-that pile of neurons
tucked away in my brain. Instead

I send my son to Barcelona to study art,
architecture, the nuances of Spanish
and Catalán—dreams-spires of melted homes,

strange obelisks of spotted color cut cross-wise
into her backdrop of terracottas and ochres.
There he'll find room for a conscience

to grow. He'll walk the hidden paths
of Gaudí's imagination, tackle the Iberian sun
to box his perceptions in cubist tradition,

unleash the Miró of his expectations.
I wish I could see it, but I am here
writing a poem about letting go, about seeing

his face on a thousand mornings
each new-found and distinct
teaching me the rules of time

for the day our times will be separated
by six steps of longitude, when freedom and restraint
will battle side by side, for generations.

The Gift

My friend and I watch
our daughters bud breasts,
change faces with young women

who bear more resemblance to us.
Our lives have taken a strange turn.
We no longer recognize them

and yield to the clarity of a late-October
sky, watch spirits dance in twirling leaves.
Everything is changing; the new replaces the old,

and we go dancing, dancing, as if
we never walked those unmitigated miles,
or gave ourselves to a future

we'd be surprised to find.
In this freedom there is mortality,
but the burden has lightened.

Our daughters' backs grow strong.
For a brief moment now
we regard one another blindly.

There is no script for the perfect gift.

Shadows

Now You Are Here

Now you are here, in the present,
as I drift into afternoon sleep.
My stomach aching, I have thrown in the towel

on being respectable (office hours
have dwindled). I've drunk Fernet:
full of secret ingredients, one of them

belladonna. I hold myself beneath a pillow
blanket, wondering if this means
fever. My arms turn into lead

and detach; eyelids also refuse to rise
so I can't see you now embracing me
repeating those three words—

I love you. I love you. I love you—
until I can't answer back
only struggle with illusions I create

to fill your absence, my penance
for doing anything but loving you
as the ashes of respectability

darken an afternoon sky.

I Write on Air

Through all hours of the night,
my wife asleep, pencils and pens
strewn in darkness about the house,

tablets unopened, stray scraps
used as bookmarks, falling from tables
and swept into corners.

The record of my thoughts is atmosphere,
the mix of gasses we must breathe
on which I write nightly, forefinger tracing

the shapes I learned in third grade,
a nunlike cursive flowing without
resistance of paper, pondering, or rewrite.

My best stories perambulate as phantoms
in a materially-impressed world.
I cannot recall them; they penetrate loneliness

and resurface in uncensored décor,
invisible and timely, unending
their story of despair.

My Life Plays Constantly Before Me

My life plays constantly before me.
By the time I die I'll have it memorized,
nothing new or surprising

to pop out of the woodwork
or raise a faded banner. I forever see
my parents' wedding; I know the scent

of my father's hair, and the soft scents
of immigrant cooking,
the way they passed me around

in bilingual chatter. And then our house.
It had no beginning, a stark shell
of buff-colored brick on a busy bend

of black road that began in red brick.
I live with those both dead and alive,
watch them in unassuming conversation,

daily silhouettes that shadow my contemporary
drama, a necessary translation of one life
into those that came before it,

still lifes still alive, each gesture
a masterpiece to be studied and memorized
in endless salutation.

Snapping Turtles

Cool woods in early April, looking
for birds high in the trees—
a canopy still bared

except for the sounds of blue jays calling,
dainty woodpeckers filling the void.
Before me a glassy pond catches

the sun—something I hadn't considered.
A lizard breaks the surface. No,
a pliosaur, straight from Loch Ness.

I watch a leathery, sharp-nailed hand
reach out of the water, then flap down,
roll over, to reveal an armored case.

My binoculars add breadth, outsize
this monster. Now there are two
tumbling over one another in shallower

water. Semi-submerged, they frighten away
the reason I came: to unveil new heights
of flight, not the shadowy depths

of my unknowns.

Shadows of Light

If, as my daughter said, angels sleep
on clouds, then I see them in slumber
below me: their luminous heads tucked gently
into cartilaginous arms, torsos curving like
capital G's. Their rest is the rest

of eternity. Storms pass over, and they rise
with the newest mist. Some are guardians,
others blow trumpets at dawn, but all have looked down

on Earth's life of folly, neither judging nor wanting.
Theirs is a life of omniscience
and deliverance; they've watched every settlement
with painstaking perspicacity, offering their shadows
of light to stir the souls of the dying.

In some way they've done their job.
Though we have taken their space, flying above
in loud, earthen metal, we are too preoccupied
to steal their work. And so they

are sleeping, relinquished
to us. But angels' dreams are heavy,
pulling them down and weighing their buoyancy
like our conscience, with its burden of history.

Upon Visiting FDR's Grave

A block of black granite
bearing his name
sits unadorned, surrounded
by thick hedge.

November silence, the few visitors
astonished to see the *Roosevelt*—
rose garden—still blooming,
a rich mulch piled up

about the thorny stems
announcing a separated space,
flip side of the square lawn
in which he lay. A planet

lies buried beneath him, a host
of naked trees hovers over
the solace of Hyde Park, its modest mansion
now approachable, and out back

the long hill he rode in snow,
its lookout to Hudson Valley wild.
Inside, a case of stuffed birds he'd shot
and labeled, just one of each

according to his father's rule,
a shrine to responsibility and reverence
for all those species, each native
to these lovely woods, a thing

one could not understand, the result
of earth's hardest work, there only
for us to tame, never master.

For Josephine Z.

Dirt rises in dark piles, untidy protuberances
above autumn's green lawn: earth
inside-out, an eyesore for us

who prefer to pat it into place,
arrange our thoughts around florals
and evergreens. *This brown powder*

has no power over us. Its depth increases
beneath our feet; its substance rises
in unwanted chemical forms.

Some of it we plunder, mold, mix
to suit our whims. It gives us carbon, concrete,
steel; ochre, sienna, gold dust; pebbles

to pick up on the beach. And we give back?
One day. Standing on a chilly hilltop,
exiting the airless chapel to watch the trees

tremble to hide our human stories
as the coffin sinks into her pit
of shadow, and we turn back

to our lives of otherworldly atmosphere,
its tended reach of green.

Requiem for an Old Friend

(for Stella Mihajlovic Bauer)

The first time you left
as I grew out of childhood;
the plants you'd given me
dried up; my plot grassed over
as yours grew smaller
from the weight of your years.

The second time I left
and forgot the smell of dirt,
its seasons, and gifts that grow
from gifts. I rushed to the spirit
and left my steps behind
to freeze, fill, then disappear.

So now you've died at ninety-four
and made me remember you
even after I've left
so many lives, given two new;

and lie resurrected
from my yard, and yours—
where I lay throwing little rocks at the sky
full of falling bats, and stars.

Wisława

I see her walking in Kraków's immense
Medieval square, wearing a cocked hat
to balance her tilted face.

She seems to take in everything
at once, walking slowly and alone,
welcoming the oblivion.

I sit in a city I once visited
in another time, when its buildings
were black, its streetcars shooting sparks

that lit scenes similar
to my Pittsburgh home.
I swooned in time travel, felt layers awaken

around my heart, heard ancestors' footsteps
disappearing around corners, their hands
barely touching my shoulders.

And now here is Wisława Szymborska
strolling through two world wars,
controversial governments

and a university that houses
her Nobel medal, as if this were merely
God's gift, long shadows in early evening

at the end of another Polish summer.

After Whitman's "Vigil Strange I Kept On the Field One Night"

Each soldier
of the tens of thousands who lay
in blind earth, made invisible

by her loving palm, their lives
blotted by an arcing shadow;
each becomes a brief thought

a pinpoint along a flat plan
laid out on the stained tables
of generals, captains, presidents.

We are here to play taps,
raise flags, and weep tears
at orchestrated ceremonies

too removed from the battle
to have much significance
except in the heads of those planners.

Only Whitman can see
each death, each face
at once glorified and destroyed—

random meetings on a stage
that has no props, nothing of life
as anyone cares to know it

only what passes between two sets
of eyes: lightning realizations that death
is not foolery, but the planning of it

is, a forfeiting of those stunning
orbs of light
to a dark, uncaring sky.

Following the Sandy Hook School Massacre

For the first time I believe my hand
hovers over a useless alphabet
under inadequate light.
For the first time I hear the voices

of strangers on the other side,
their shadowy forms taking up more space
than the sunny air, their voices
speaking a language read only

by silence. This is the first time
no one can take sides, nor condescend
with confident offers of help.
This is the first time

we are bound by a place
that will bear us all
under a dome that finally gives
a hint of the sacred, that engulfs

all knowledge, wisdom, and days
and replaces them with stalled beginnings.

God Lives in the Heart of a Tree

God lives in the heart
of a tree. He grows there
before our house, hovering over
traffic, dropping branches
during storms, buckling under snow,
budding red at the end of March.

The electric company prunes Him
every so many years; sanitation trucks
tear at His twigs. Our daughter poses in His shadow
on her first day of school. He stands silent
as our government wages war.

He is busy, as usual, dividing cells
to grow imperceptibly. His leaves change
while we are at work, drop without
fanfare, then blow away to fertilize
His alter-egos. The arborist says

He'll last about another ten years
before carpenter ants widen the furrow
they've gnawed apart. But we will not notice
that anything has changed. The tree will be gone
and we will plant another at the end

of a busy summer day. At first we'll water
and till around it, then forget it for faith
that it will keep its steady promise
something in the backs of our minds
that we neither care for nor wish

would go away: a designated space
for the uninvented, unhurried, unlikeness
of our lives.

Made in the USA
Middletown, DE
20 April 2017